THE SOFT RESET
Planner

96-day guide to reset your mind and body

ERICKA WILLIAMS
CLASSY CLIMB

The Soft Reset
Planner

96-day guide to reset your mind and body

Name: ◊◊◊

Email: ◊◊◊

Copyright© 2021 Ericka Williams. All rights reserved.
Published by SW Investments TX LLC
978-1-7342082-2-1 Unique ISBN

All rights reserved, including the right to reproduce this book or portions thereof in any form whatsoever. For information, address the publisher.

All rights reserved. This book or parts thereof may not be reproduced in any form, stored in any retrieval system, or transmitted in any form by any means—electronic, mechanical, photocopy, recording, or otherwise—without prior written permission of the publisher, except as provided by United States of America copyright law. For permission requests, write to the publisher, at "Attention: Permissions Coordinator," at the address below:
Ericka.s.williams@gmail.com

LET'S MAKE SELF REFLECTION A HABIT

As you write in your journal check off the boxes to celebrate your consistency.

WEEK

	M	T	W	T	F	S	S
1	☐	☐	☐	☐	☐	☐	☐
2	☐	☐	☐	☐	☐	☐	☐
3	☐	☐	☐	☐	☐	☐	☐
4	☐	☐	☐	☐	☐	☐	☐
5	☐	☐	☐	☐	☐	☐	☐
6	☐	☐	☐	☐	☐	☐	☐
7	☐	☐	☐	☐	☐	☐	☐
8	☐	☐	☐	☐	☐	☐	☐
9	☐	☐	☐	☐	☐	☐	☐
10	☐	☐	☐	☐	☐	☐	☐
11	☐	☐	☐	☐	☐	☐	☐
12	☐	☐	☐	☐	☐	☐	☐

This planner is the perfect tool for anyone looking to simplify their life and achieve their goals. I created this planner as we move forward into a new year where "LESS is MORE". My goal for this planner is to help you reach your goals without the anxiety that comes with our "busy" society.

Whether you're looking to get more in touch with your inner peace or create tangible action steps towards your goals, the Soft Reset Planner has got you covered! I would love to hear your feedback on how this journal helped you in gain more control over yourself and dreams.

—Ericka Williams

M ☐ T ☐ W ☐ T ☐ F ☐ S ☐ S ☐

DATE : ____ ____ ____

DAILY
Check-in

∞∞∞∞∞∞∞∞∞∞∞∞∞∞∞∞∞∞∞∞∞∞∞∞∞∞∞∞∞∞∞∞∞∞∞∞∞

Today I am grateful for...
_____
_____
_____
_____

Today I'm looking forward to...
_____
_____
_____

How do you feel today?:

- ☐ Happy
- ☐ Sad
- ☐ Stressed
- ☐ Energized
- ☐ Tired
- ☐ Stressed
- ☐ Fearful
- ☐ Angry

- ☐ Peaceful
- ☐ Disappointed
- ☐ Anxious
- ☐ Annoyed
- ☐ Hopeful
- ☐ Calm
- ☐ Productive
- ☐ Excited

- ☐ Negative
- ☐ Strong
- ☐ Inspired
- ☐ Thankful
- ☐ Loving
- ☐ Loved
- ☐ _____
- ☐ _____

What happened?
_____
_____

Things that went well today?

1. _____
2. _____
3. _____
4. _____

M T W T F S S
☐ ☐ ☐ ☐ ☐ ☐ ☐

DAILY
Check-in

DATE : ____ ____ ____

∞∞∞

I am grateful for...
_____
_____
_____
_____

What lessons did you learn today?
_____
_____
_____
_____
_____
_____

What ways did you move your body today?:
_____
_____
_____
_____

What are you looking forward to tomorrow?:
_____
_____
_____
_____

♡ Self Care Time: Take a relaxing bubble bath, while
   listening to a peaceful song or meditation.

☐ Task Completed

M T W T F S S
☐ ☐ ☐ ☐ ☐ ☐ ☐

DAILY *Check-in*

DATE : ____ ____ ____

What is the best thing that happened today or yesterday?
_____
_____
_____
_____

Positive Affirmation: I am...
_____
_____
_____

How do you feel today?:

- ☐ Happy
- ☐ Sad
- ☐ Stressed
- ☐ Energized
- ☐ Tired
- ☐ Stressed
- ☐ Fearful
- ☐ Angry

- ☐ Peaceful
- ☐ Disappointed
- ☐ Anxious
- ☐ Annoyed
- ☐ Hopeful
- ☐ Calm
- ☐ Productive
- ☐ Excited

- ☐ Negative
- ☐ Strong
- ☐ Inspired
- ☐ Thankful
- ☐ Loving
- ☐ Loved
- ☐ _____
- ☐ _____

What happened?
_____
_____
_____

What do you want to celebrate about yourself today?

1. _____
2. _____
3. _____
4. _____

M	T	W	T	F	S	S
☐	☐	☐	☐	☐	☐	☐

DAILY
Check-in

DATE : ____ ____ ____

∞∞

Intention for the day:
_____
_____
_____
_____

Is there anything that you're holding onto that you need to release?
_____
_____
_____
_____
_____
_____

Look around your space, what is an item that brings you joy?
_____
_____
_____
_____
_____
_____
_____

Your space is a reflection of you. Pick up a new item that brings you joy. What will you purchase?
_____
_____
_____
_____

M T W T F S S
☐ ☐ ☐ ☐ ☐ ☐ ☐

DAILY
Check-in

DATE : ____ ____ ____

◇◇

I am grateful for...
_____
_____
_____

Today I will:
_____
_____
_____
_____

Notes//Reminders

I'm proud of myself for...
_____
_____
_____
_____
_____
_____

M T W T F S S
☐ ☐ ☐ ☐ ☐ ☐ ☐

DAILY
Check-in

DATE : ____ ____ ____

I am grateful for...

_____
_____
_____
_____

What's something that brought you joy today?

_____
_____
_____
_____

One micro goal that I acomplisehd today:

_____
_____
_____
_____
_____
_____

Big Wins/ Lessons

_____
_____
_____
_____
_____
_____

M T W T F S S
☐ ☐ ☐ ☐ ☐ ☐ ☐

DAILY
Check-in

DATE : ____ ____ ____

❝ When the whole world is silent, even one voice becomes powerful.
 - Malala Yousafzai

What's the biggest obstacle that you're currently facing?
What's one small step you can take to overcome
this obstacle?
_____
_____
_____
_____
_____
_____
_____
_____
_____
_____

Wellness commitment:
This week I will take better care of my body by:
_____
_____
_____

Even if life gets busy one thing I can do to take care of
myself is:
_____
_____
_____

Feeling Anxious? Did you know that moving your body can
help relieve stress? That's right exercise releases
endorphins which triggers a positive feeling in the body.

Did you move your body today? (a 20 minute walk counts)

☐   ☐
YES NO

Reflect

Self Care Time: Take a relaxing bubble bath, while listening to a peaceful song or meditation.

Task Completed

M ☐ T ☐ W ☐ T ☐ F ☐ S ☐ S ☐

DAILY
Check-in

DATE : ____ ____ ____

∞∞∞∞∞∞∞∞∞∞∞∞∞∞∞∞∞∞∞∞∞∞∞∞∞∞∞∞∞∞∞∞

I am grateful for...
_____
_____
_____
_____

Today I'm proud that I...
_____
_____
_____
_____

How do you feel today?:

☐ Happy   ☐ Peaceful   ☐ Negative
☐ Sad   ☐ Disappointed   ☐ Strong
☐ Stressed   ☐ Anxious   ☐ Inspired
☐ Energized   ☐ Annoyed   ☐ Thankful
☐ Tired   ☐ Hopeful   ☐ Loving
☐ Stressed   ☐ Calm   ☐ Loved
☐ Fearful   ☐ Productive   ☐ _____
☐ Angry   ☐ Excited   ☐ _____

What happened?
_____
_____
_____

Things that went well today?
1. _____
_____
2. _____
_____
3. _____
_____

M T W T F S S
☐ ☐ ☐ ☐ ☐ ☐ ☐

DAILY
Check-in

DATE : ____ ____ ____

◇◇

I am grateful for...
_____
_____
_____
_____

What lessons did you learn today?
_____
_____
_____
_____
_____
_____

What ways did you move your body today?:
_____
_____
_____
_____

What are you looking forward to tomorrow?:
_____
_____
_____
_____

♡   Energy Boost: If you're feeling low on energy vitamin B12 helps transform the food you eat into energy that your cells can use. Give vitamin B12 a try!

M T W T F S S
☐ ☐ ☐ ☐ ☐ ☐ ☐

DAILY
Check-in

DATE : ____ ____ ____

What is the best thing that happened today or yesterday?
_____
_____
_____
_____

Positive Affirmation: I am...
_____
_____
_____

How do you feel today?:

- ☐ Happy
- ☐ Sad
- ☐ Stressed
- ☐ Energized
- ☐ Tired
- ☐ Stressed
- ☐ Fearful
- ☐ Angry

- ☐ Peaceful
- ☐ Disappointed
- ☐ Anxious
- ☐ Annoyed
- ☐ Hopeful
- ☐ Calm
- ☐ Productive
- ☐ Excited

- ☐ Negative
- ☐ Strong
- ☐ Inspired
- ☐ Thankful
- ☐ Loving
- ☐ Loved
- ☐ _____
- ☐ _____

What happened?
_____
_____
_____

The words I'd like to live by are . . .

1. _____
2. _____
3. _____
4. _____

M T W T F S S
☐ ☐ ☐ ☐ ☐ ☐ ☐

DAILY
Check-in

DATE : ____ ____ ____

Intention for the day:
___
___
___
___

Am I waking up in the morning ready to take on the day?
___
___
___
___
___
___

If my body could talk, it would say . . .
___
___
___
___
___
___
___
___

What'ssomething that will bring you joy this week?
___
___
___

M T W T F S S
☐ ☐ ☐ ☐ ☐ ☐ ☐

DAILY
Check-in

DATE : ____ ____ ____

◇◇

I am grateful for...

_____
_____
_____

Today I will:

_____
_____
_____
_____

Notes//Reminders

┌───┐
│   │
│   │
│   │
│   │
│   │
│   │
│   │
└───┘

I'm proud of myself for...

_____
_____
_____
_____
_____
_____

M	T	W	T	F	S	S
☐	☐	☐	☐	☐	☐	☐

DAILY
Check-in

DATE : ____ ____ ____

I am grateful for...

_____
_____
_____
_____

My favorite way to spend the day is . . .

_____
_____
_____
_____
_____

One micro goal that I acomplisehd today:

_____
_____
_____
_____
_____
_____

Big Wins/ Lessons

_____
_____
_____
_____
_____
_____

M T W T F S S
☐ ☐ ☐ ☐ ☐ ☐ ☐

DATE : ____ ____ ____

DAILY
Check-in

> **Once we believe in ourselves, we can risk curiosity, wonder, spontaneous delight, or any experiences that reveals the human spirit.- E.E. Cummings**

What did you say yes to this week that you probably should have said no to?

_____
_____
_____
_____
_____
_____
_____
_____
_____
_____

Wellness commitment:
This week I will take better care of my body by:
_____
_____

Even if life gets busy one thing I can do to take care of myself is:
_____
_____

How many times did you move your body this week? (a 20 minute walk counts)
_____
_____

Reflect

Self Care Time: Sit in the grass and watch the clouds float by.

☐ Task Completed

M ☐ T ☐ W ☐ T ☐ F ☐ S ☐ S ☐

DATE : ____ ____ ____

DAILY
Check-in

∞∞∞∞∞∞∞∞∞∞∞∞∞∞∞∞∞∞∞∞∞∞∞∞∞∞∞∞∞∞∞

Today I am grateful for...
_____
_____
_____
_____

Today I'm looking forward to...
_____
_____
_____

How do you feel today?:

- ☐ Happy
- ☐ Sad
- ☐ Stressed
- ☐ Energized
- ☐ Tired
- ☐ Stressed
- ☐ Fearful
- ☐ Angry

- ☐ Peaceful
- ☐ Disappointed
- ☐ Anxious
- ☐ Annoyed
- ☐ Hopeful
- ☐ Calm
- ☐ Productive
- ☐ Excited

- ☐ Negative
- ☐ Strong
- ☐ Inspired
- ☐ Thankful
- ☐ Loving
- ☐ Loved
- ☐ _____
- ☐ _____

What happened?
_____
_____
_____

Things that went well today?

1. _____
_____
2. _____
_____
3. _____
_____
4. _____
_____
_____

M	T	W	T	F	S	S
☐	☐	☐	☐	☐	☐	☐

DAILY
Check-in

DATE : ____ ____ ____

◇◇◇

I am grateful for...

_____
_____
_____
_____

What lessons did you learn today?

_____
_____
_____
_____
_____
_____

What keeps you grounded?

_____
_____
_____
_____

What are you looking forward to tomorrow?:

_____
_____
_____
_____

♡ Self Care Time: Start or finish your day with a 10 minute yoga video.

☐ Task Completed

M T W T F S S
☐ ☐ ☐ ☐ ☐ ☐ ☐

DAILY
Check-in

DATE : ____ ____ ____

What is the best thing that happened today or yesterday?
_____
_____
_____
_____

Positive Affirmation: I am...
_____
_____

How do you feel today?:

- ☐ Happy
- ☐ Sad
- ☐ Stressed
- ☐ Energized
- ☐ Tired
- ☐ Stressed
- ☐ Fearful
- ☐ Angry

- ☐ Peaceful
- ☐ Disappointed
- ☐ Anxious
- ☐ Annoyed
- ☐ Hopeful
- ☐ Calm
- ☐ Productive
- ☐ Excited

- ☐ Negative
- ☐ Strong
- ☐ Inspired
- ☐ Thankful
- ☐ Loving
- ☐ Loved
- ☐ _____
- ☐ _____

What happened?
_____
_____
_____

What do you want to celebrate about yourself today?

1. _____
2. _____
3. _____
4. _____

M T W T F S S
☐ ☐ ☐ ☐ ☐ ☐ ☐

DAILY
Check-in

DATE : ____ ____ ____

Intention for the day:
_____
_____
_____
_____

What makes you feel energised and refreshed?
_____
_____
_____
_____
_____
_____

What's your favourite self-care activity? Why do you enjoy it so much?
_____
_____
_____
_____
_____
_____
_____

What's something that will bring you joy this week?
_____
_____
_____
_____

M T W T F S S
☐ ☐ ☐ ☐ ☐ ☐ ☐

DAILY
Check-in

DATE : ____ ____ ____

❝ *We are products of our past, but we don't have to be prisoners of it.*
   - Rick Warren

I am grateful for...
_____
_____
_____

Today I will:
_____
_____
_____
_____

Notes//Reminders

I'm proud of myself for...
_____
_____
_____
_____
_____
_____
_____

M T W T F S S
☐ ☐ ☐ ☐ ☐ ☐ ☐

DAILY
Check-in

DATE : ____ ____ ____

◇◇

I am grateful for...
_____
_____
_____
_____

Who do you most enjoy spending time with? Why is that?
_____
_____
_____
_____
_____

One micro goal that I acomplisehd today:
_____
_____
_____
_____
_____
_____

Big Wins/ Lessons
_____
_____
_____
_____
_____
_____
_____

M T W T F S S
☐ ☐ ☐ ☐ ☐ ☐ ☐

DAILY
Check-in

DATE : ____ ____ ____

> *The swiftest way to triple your success is to double your investment in personal development.. - Robin Sharma*

What did you say yes to this week that you probably should have said no to?
_____
_____
_____
_____
_____
_____
_____
_____
_____
_____

Wellness commitment:
This week I will take better care of my body by:
_____
_____

Even if life gets busy one thing I can do to take care of myself is:
_____
_____

How many times did you move your body this week? (a 20 minute walk counts)
_____
_____

Reflect

Self Care Time: Pick or buy a bouquet of fresh flowers.

☐ Task Completed

M ☐ T ☐ W ☐ T ☐ F ☐ S ☐ S ☐

DAILY
Check-in

DATE : ____ ____ ____

Today I am grateful for...
_____
_____
_____
_____

Today I'm looking forward to...
_____
_____
_____

How do you feel today?:

- ☐ Happy
- ☐ Sad
- ☐ Stressed
- ☐ Energized
- ☐ Tired
- ☐ Stressed
- ☐ Fearful
- ☐ Angry

- ☐ Peaceful
- ☐ Disappointed
- ☐ Anxious
- ☐ Annoyed
- ☐ Hopeful
- ☐ Calm
- ☐ Productive
- ☐ Excited

- ☐ Negative
- ☐ Strong
- ☐ Inspired
- ☐ Thankful
- ☐ Loving
- ☐ Loved
- ☐ _____
- ☐ _____

What happened?
_____
_____
_____

3 things I've overcame recently that I'm proud of:
1. _____
_____
_____
2. _____
_____
_____
3. _____
_____

M T W T F S S
☐ ☐ ☐ ☐ ☐ ☐ ☐

DAILY
Check-in

DATE : ____ ____ ____

∞∞

I am grateful for...
_____
_____
_____
_____

What lessons did you learn today?
_____
_____
_____
_____
_____
_____

What ways did you move your body today?:
_____
_____
_____
_____

What are you looking forward to tomorrow?:
_____
_____
_____
_____

♡   Self Care Time: Do a 10 minute meditation today.

☐   Task Completed

M T W T F S S
☐ ☐ ☐ ☐ ☐ ☐ ☐

DAILY
Check-in

DATE : ____ ____ ____

How can you simplify your life in a small way today?
_____
_____
_____
_____

Positive Affirmation: I am...
_____
_____
_____

How do you feel today?:

- ☐ Happy
- ☐ Sad
- ☐ Stressed
- ☐ Energized
- ☐ Tired
- ☐ Stressed
- ☐ Fearful
- ☐ Angry

- ☐ Peaceful
- ☐ Disappointed
- ☐ Anxious
- ☐ Annoyed
- ☐ Hopeful
- ☐ Calm
- ☐ Productive
- ☐ Excited

- ☐ Negative
- ☐ Strong
- ☐ Inspired
- ☐ Thankful
- ☐ Loving
- ☐ Loved
- ☐ _____
- ☐ _____

What happened?
_____
_____
_____

What do you want to celebrate about yourself today?

1. _____
2. _____
3. _____
4. _____

M T W T F S S
☐ ☐ ☐ ☐ ☐ ☐ ☐

DAILY
Check-in

DATE :

Intention for the day:
_____
_____
_____
_____

What from your past are you still holding onto that you need to release?
_____
_____
_____
_____
_____
_____

What do you wish you did more of?
_____
_____
_____
_____
_____
_____

When do you feel the most at peace?
_____
_____
_____
_____
_____

M T W T F S S
☐ ☐ ☐ ☐ ☐ ☐ ☐

DAILY
Check-in

DATE : ____ ____ ____

> **Growth is never by mere chance; it is the result of forces working together.- James Cash Penney, founder, JC Penney**

I am grateful for...
_____
_____
_____

Today I will:
_____
_____
_____
_____

Notes//Reminders

I'm proud of myself for...
_____
_____
_____
_____
_____
_____

M T W T F S S
☐ ☐ ☐ ☐ ☐ ☐ ☐

DAILY
Check-in

DATE : ___ ___ ___

I am grateful for...

_____
_____
_____
_____

What challenge are you currently facing?

_____
_____
_____
_____
_____

Two micro goals that I acomplisehd today:

☐ _____
_____
_____
_____
☐ _____
_____
_____
_____

Big Wins/ Lessons

_____
_____
_____
_____
_____
_____

M T W T F S S
☐ ☐ ☐ ☐ ☐ ☐ ☐

DAILY
Check-in

DATE : ____ ____ ____

> *Play by the rules, but be ferocious. — Phil Knight, founder, Nike*

Are there any new boundaries that you need to put in place?
_____
_____
_____
_____
_____
_____
_____
_____
_____
_____

Wellness commitment:
This week I will take better care of my body by:
_____
_____

Even if life gets busy one thing I can do to take care of myself is:
_____
_____

How many times did you move your body this week? (a 20 minute walk counts)
_____
_____

Reflect

Self Care Time: Make a phone or coffee date with a friend you haven't seen in awhile.

Task Completed

M T W T F S S
☐ ☐ ☐ ☐ ☐ ☐ ☐

DAILY
Check-in

DATE : ____ ____ ____

Today I am grateful for...
_____
_____
_____
_____

Today I'm looking forward to...
_____
_____
_____

How do you feel today?:

☐ Happy   ☐ Peaceful   ☐ Negative
☐ Sad   ☐ Disappointed   ☐ Strong
☐ Stressed   ☐ Anxious   ☐ Inspired
☐ Energized   ☐ Annoyed   ☐ Thankful
☐ Tired   ☐ Hopeful   ☐ Loving
☐ Stressed   ☐ Calm   ☐ Loved
☐ Fearful   ☐ Productive   ☐ _____
☐ Angry   ☐ Excited   ☐ _____

What happened?
_____
_____
_____

What things are you avoiding dealing with?
_____
_____
_____
_____
_____
_____
_____

M T W T F S S
☐ ☐ ☐ ☐ ☐ ☐ ☐

DAILY
Check-in

DATE : ____ ____ ____

◇◇

I am grateful for...
_____
_____
_____
_____

What inspires you?
_____
_____
_____
_____
_____
_____
_____

Make a list of 5 things that make you happy?
_____
_____
_____
_____
_____

What are you looking forward to tomorrow?:
_____
_____
_____
_____

♡ Self Care Time: Get out in the sun and go for a long walk.

☐ Task Completed

M T W T F S S
☐ ☐ ☐ ☐ ☐ ☐ ☐

DAILY
Check-in

DATE : ____ ____ ____

◇◇◇

What is the best thing that happened today or yesterday?
_____
_____
_____
_____

Pick one positive word you'd like to focus on today
_____
_____

How do you feel today?:

☐ Happy   ☐ Peaceful   ☐ Negative
☐ Sad   ☐ Disappointed   ☐ Strong
☐ Stressed   ☐ Anxious   ☐ Inspired
☐ Energized   ☐ Annoyed   ☐ Thankful
☐ Tired   ☐ Hopeful   ☐ Loving
☐ Stressed   ☐ Calm   ☐ Loved
☐ Fearful   ☐ Productive   ☐ _____
☐ Angry   ☐ Excited   ☐ _____

What happened?
_____
_____
_____

What do you want to celebrate about yourself today?

1. _____
2. _____
3. _____
4. _____

M T W T F S S
☐ ☐ ☐ ☐ ☐ ☐ ☐

DAILY
Check-in

DATE : ___ ___ ___

◇◇

Intention for the day:
_____
_____
_____
_____

What makes you feel energised and refreshed?
_____
_____
_____
_____
_____
_____

What's your favourite self-care activity? Why do you enjoy it so much?
_____
_____
_____
_____
_____
_____

What's something that will bring you joy this week?
_____
_____
_____
_____

M T W T F S S
☐ ☐ ☐ ☐ ☐ ☐ ☐

DAILY
Check-in

DATE : ____ ____ ____

I am grateful for...
_____
_____
_____

Today I will:
_____
_____
_____
_____

Notes//Reminders

I'm proud of myself for...
_____
_____
_____
_____
_____
_____

M T W T F S S
☐ ☐ ☐ ☐ ☐ ☐ ☐

DAILY
Check-in

DATE : ____ ____ ____

I am grateful for...
_____
_____
_____
_____

Is there anything that you want to let go of in this season?
_____
_____
_____
_____

One micro goal that I acomplisehd today:
_____
_____
_____
_____
_____

Big Wins/ Lessons
_____
_____
_____
_____
_____
_____

M T W T F S S
☐ ☐ ☐ ☐ ☐ ☐ ☐

DAILY
Check-in

DATE : ____ ____ ____

> **If you don't make the time to work on creating the life you want, you're eventually going to be forced to spend a lot of time dealing with a life you don't want. -Kevin Ngo**

On a scale of 1-10 how satisfied are you with your life? What can you add that can make you more satisfied?

_____
_____
_____
_____
_____
_____
_____
_____
_____
_____

Wellness commitment:
This week I will take better care of my body by:
_____
_____
_____

Even if life gets busy one thing I can do to take care of myself is:
_____
_____

How many times did you move your body this week? (a 20 minute walk counts)
_____
_____

Reflect

Self Care Time: Start a cycle of encouragement. Tell someone near you what you appreciate about them.

☐ Task Completed

M ☐ T ☐ W ☐ T ☐ F ☐ S ☐ S ☐

DAILY
Check-in

DATE : ____ ____ ____

∞∞

Today I am grateful for...

_____
_____
_____
_____

Today I'm looking forward to...

_____
_____
_____

How do you feel today?:

- ☐ Happy
- ☐ Sad
- ☐ Stressed
- ☐ Energized
- ☐ Tired
- ☐ Stressed
- ☐ Fearful
- ☐ Angry

- ☐ Peaceful
- ☐ Disappointed
- ☐ Anxious
- ☐ Annoyed
- ☐ Hopeful
- ☐ Calm
- ☐ Productive
- ☐ Excited

- ☐ Negative
- ☐ Strong
- ☐ Inspired
- ☐ Thankful
- ☐ Loving
- ☐ Loved
- ☐ _____
- ☐ _____

What happened?
_____
_____
_____

List 4 things that are going well in your life.

1. _____
_____
2. _____
_____
3. _____
_____
4. _____
_____

M T W T F S S
☐ ☐ ☐ ☐ ☐ ☐ ☐

DAILY
Check-in

DATE : ____ ____ ____

I love myself because...
_____
_____
_____
_____

Who are you at your core?
_____
_____
_____
_____
_____
_____

If someone described you, what would they say?
_____
_____
_____
_____

What are you looking forward to tomorrow?:
_____
_____
_____
_____

♡ Self Care Time: When you wake up in the morning, get in the habit of making your first thought a positive one

☐ Task Completed

M ☐ T ☐ W ☐ T ☐ F ☐ S ☐ S ☐

DAILY
Check-in

DATE : ____ ____ ____

∞∞∞∞∞∞∞∞∞∞∞∞∞∞∞∞∞∞∞∞∞∞∞∞∞∞∞∞∞∞∞∞∞∞∞∞

What is the best thing that happened today or yesterday?
_____
_____
_____
_____

Positive Affirmation: I am...
_____
_____
_____

How do you feel today?:

- ☐ Happy
- ☐ Sad
- ☐ Stressed
- ☐ Energized
- ☐ Tired
- ☐ Stressed
- ☐ Fearful
- ☐ Angry

- ☐ Peaceful
- ☐ Disappointed
- ☐ Anxious
- ☐ Annoyed
- ☐ Hopeful
- ☐ Calm
- ☐ Productive
- ☐ Excited

- ☐ Negative
- ☐ Strong
- ☐ Inspired
- ☐ Thankful
- ☐ Loving
- ☐ Loved
- ☐ _____
- ☐ _____

What happened?
_____
_____

What is a challenge that you have overcome recently that you need to give yourself credit for?
_____
_____
_____
_____
_____
_____

M T W T F S S
☐ ☐ ☐ ☐ ☐ ☐ ☐

DAILY
Check-in

DATE : ____ ____

∞∞

Intention for the day:
_____
_____
_____
_____

What is your favorite way to start the day?
_____
_____
_____
_____
_____

What are some comfortable aspects of your life that you sometimes take for granted?
_____
_____
_____
_____
_____
_____
_____

What excites you about your future?
_____
_____
_____
_____
_____

M ☐ T ☐ W ☐ T ☐ F ☐ S ☐ S ☐

DAILY
Check-in

DATE : ____ ____ ____

I am grateful for...
_____
_____
_____

Today I will:
_____
_____
_____
_____

Notes//Reminders

What do you need to focus on less?
_____
_____
_____
_____
_____
_____
_____

M T W T F S S
☐ ☐ ☐ ☐ ☐ ☐ ☐

DAILY
Check-in

DATE : ___ ___ ___

◇◇

I am grateful for...
_____
_____
_____
_____

What is an area of your life that could use more organization?
_____
_____
_____
_____

What's one of your favorite compliments that you've recieved?
_____
_____
_____
_____
_____
_____

Big Wins/lessons so far this week
_____
_____
_____
_____
_____
_____

M T W T F S S
☐ ☐ ☐ ☐ ☐ ☐ ☐

DAILY
Check-in

DATE : ____ ____ ____

> **The tragedy in life doesn't lie in not reaching your goal. The tragedy lies in having no goal to reach. -Benjamin Mays**

What's something you've enjoyed about your work recently?
_____
_____
_____
_____
_____
_____
_____
_____
_____
_____

Wellness commitment:
This week I will take better care of my body by:
_____
_____
_____

Even if life gets busy one thing I can do to take care of myself is:
_____
_____
_____

How many times did you move your body this week? (a 20 minute walk counts)
_____
_____

Reflect

Self Care Time: Give yourself a social media break for at least one day this week.

☐ Task Completed

M T W T F S S
☐ ☐ ☐ ☐ ☐ ☐ ☐

DAILY
Check-in

DATE : ____ ____ ____

Today I am grateful for...
_____
_____
_____
_____

Today I'm looking forward to...
_____
_____
_____

How do you feel today?:

- ☐ Happy
- ☐ Sad
- ☐ Stressed
- ☐ Energized
- ☐ Tired
- ☐ Stressed
- ☐ Fearful
- ☐ Angry

- ☐ Peaceful
- ☐ Disappointed
- ☐ Anxious
- ☐ Annoyed
- ☐ Hopeful
- ☐ Calm
- ☐ Productive
- ☐ Excited

- ☐ Negative
- ☐ Strong
- ☐ Inspired
- ☐ Thankful
- ☐ Loving
- ☐ Loved
- ☐ _____
- ☐ _____

What happened?
_____
_____
_____

Things that went well today?
1. _____
2. _____
3. _____
4. _____

M T W T F S S
☐ ☐ ☐ ☐ ☐ ☐ ☐

DAILY
Check-in

DATE : ___ ___ ___

I am grateful for...
_____
_____
_____
_____

What task has been weighing on your mind lately?
_____
_____
_____
_____
_____
_____

What's the biggest challenge that you're facing right now?
_____
_____
_____
_____

What are you looking forward to tomorrow?:
_____
_____
_____
_____

♡ Self Care Time: Cook a healthy meal using fresh ingredients you rarely splurge on.

☐ Task Completed

M T W T F S S
☐ ☐ ☐ ☐ ☐ ☐ ☐

DAILY
Check-in

DATE : ____ ____ ____

∞∞

What is the best thing that happened today or yesterday?
_____
_____
_____
_____

Positive Affirmation: I am...
_____
_____
_____

How do you feel today?:

☐ Happy   ☐ Peaceful   ☐ Negative
☐ Sad   ☐ Disappointed   ☐ Strong
☐ Stressed   ☐ Anxious   ☐ Inspired
☐ Energized   ☐ Annoyed   ☐ Thankful
☐ Tired   ☐ Hopeful   ☐ Loving
☐ Stressed   ☐ Calm   ☐ Loved
☐ Fearful   ☐ Productive   ☐ _____
☐ Angry   ☐ Excited   ☐ _____

What happened?
_____
_____
_____

Reflect on what you were doing this time last year
_____
_____
_____
_____
_____
_____
_____

M T W T F S S
☐ ☐ ☐ ☐ ☐ ☐ ☐

DAILY
Check-in

DATE : ____ ____ ____

Intention for the day:
_____
_____
_____
_____

Find an inspirational quote or Bible verse that speaks to you. Write it below. Why does this speak to you?
_____
_____
_____
_____
_____
_____
_____

What area of your life do you feel you've grown the most, in this season?
_____
_____
_____
_____
_____
_____
_____
_____

What's something that will bring you joy this week?
_____
_____
_____
_____

M T W T F S S
☐ ☐ ☐ ☐ ☐ ☐ ☐

DAILY
Check-in

DATE : ____ ____ ____

I am grateful for...
_____
_____
_____

Today I will:
_____
_____
_____
_____

Notes//Reminders

[   ]

I'm proud of myself for...
_____
_____
_____
_____

M T W T F S S
☐ ☐ ☐ ☐ ☐ ☐ ☐

DAILY
Check-in

DATE : _____ _____ _____

I am grateful for...
_____
_____
_____
_____

One micro goal that I acomplisehd today:
_____
_____
_____
_____

What does success mean to you?
_____
_____
_____
_____
_____
_____
_____

What advice would you give your younger self?
_____
_____
_____
_____
_____
_____
_____

M	T	W	T	F	S	S
☐	☐	☐	☐	☐	☐	☐

DAILY
Check-in

DATE : ___ ___ ___

❖❖

❝ *If you don't like something, change it. If you can't change it, change your attitude. - Maya Angelou*

What do you need more of in your life?
_____
_____
_____
_____
_____
_____
_____
_____
_____
_____

Wellness commitment:
This week I will take better care of my body by:
_____
_____

Even if life gets busy one thing I can do to take care of myself is:
_____
_____

How many times did you move your body this week? (a 20 minute walk counts)
_____
_____

Reflect

Self Care Time: Declutter an area in your home that you've been meaning to get to.

☐ Task Completed

M T W T F S S
☐ ☐ ☐ ☐ ☐ ☐ ☐

DAILY
Check-in

DATE : ____ ____ ____

Today I am grateful for...
_____
_____
_____
_____

Today I'm looking forward to...
_____
_____
_____

How do you feel today?:

- ☐ Happy
- ☐ Sad
- ☐ Stressed
- ☐ Energized
- ☐ Tired
- ☐ Stressed
- ☐ Fearful
- ☐ Angry

- ☐ Peaceful
- ☐ Disappointed
- ☐ Anxious
- ☐ Annoyed
- ☐ Hopeful
- ☐ Calm
- ☐ Productive
- ☐ Excited

- ☐ Negative
- ☐ Strong
- ☐ Inspired
- ☐ Thankful
- ☐ Loving
- ☐ Loved
- ☐ _____
- ☐ _____

What happened?
_____
_____
_____

What freedoms are you most grateful for?

1. _____
2. _____
3. _____
4. _____

M T W T F S S
☐ ☐ ☐ ☐ ☐ ☐ ☐

DAILY
Check-in

DATE : ____ ____ ____

∞∞∞∞∞∞∞∞∞∞∞∞∞∞∞∞∞∞∞∞∞∞∞∞∞∞∞∞∞∞∞∞∞∞∞

I am grateful for...
_____
_____
_____
_____

What do I procrastinate with the most?
_____
_____
_____
_____
_____
_____

What would your younger self be proud of you for today?
_____
_____
_____
_____

What are you looking forward to tomorrow?:
_____
_____
_____
_____

♡   Self Care Time: Take a mid-day nap.

☐   Task Completed

M T W T F S S
☐ ☐ ☐ ☐ ☐ ☐ ☐

DAILY
Check-in

DATE : ____ ____ ____

∞∞∞∞∞∞∞∞∞∞∞∞∞∞∞∞∞∞∞∞∞∞∞∞∞∞∞∞∞∞∞∞∞∞∞∞∞

What is the best thing that happened today or yesterday?
_____
_____
_____
_____

Positive Affirmation: I am...
_____
_____
_____

How do you feel today?:

☐ Happy   ☐ Peaceful   ☐ Negative
☐ Sad   ☐ Disappointed   ☐ Strong
☐ Stressed   ☐ Anxious   ☐ Inspired
☐ Energized   ☐ Annoyed   ☐ Thankful
☐ Tired   ☐ Hopeful   ☐ Loving
☐ Stressed   ☐ Calm   ☐ Loved
☐ Fearful   ☐ Productive   ☐ _____
☐ Angry   ☐ Excited   ☐ _____

What happened?
_____
_____
_____

What are 4 things that make you smile?
1. _____
2. _____
3. _____
4. _____

M T W T F S S
☐ ☐ ☐ ☐ ☐ ☐ ☐

DAILY
Check-in

DATE : ____ ____ ____

◇◇

Intention for the day:
_____
_____
_____
_____

Are you happy with the amount of sleep you're currently getting each night?
_____
_____
_____
_____
_____
_____

If you could have one day off to do whatever you wanted, what would you do?
_____
_____
_____
_____
_____
_____

What is a mantra that you live by?
_____
_____
_____
_____

M T W T F S S
☐ ☐ ☐ ☐ ☐ ☐ ☐

DAILY
Check-in

DATE : ____ ____ ____

◇◇

I am grateful for...
_____
_____
_____

Today I will:
_____
_____
_____
_____

Notes//Reminders

```
┌─────────────────────────────────────────┐
│                                         │
│                                         │
│                                         │
│                                         │
│                                         │
│                                         │
└─────────────────────────────────────────┘
```

If my body had a voice it would whisper…
_____
_____
_____
_____
_____
_____

M T W T F S S
☐ ☐ ☐ ☐ ☐ ☐ ☐

DAILY
Check-in

DATE : ____ ____ ____

I am grateful for...
_____
_____
_____
_____

What's something that brought you joy today?
_____
_____
_____
_____
_____

One micro goal that I acomplisehd today:
_____
_____
_____
_____
_____
_____

I forgive myself for...
_____
_____
_____
_____
_____
_____
_____

M T W T F S S
☐ ☐ ☐ ☐ ☐ ☐ ☐

DAILY
Check-in

DATE : ____ ____ ____

> **Be patient with yourself. Self-growth is tender; it's holy ground. There's no greater investment. - Stephen Covey**

I take time to care for myself by...
_____
_____
_____
_____
_____
_____
_____
_____
_____

Wellness commitment:
This week I will take better care of my body by:
_____
_____

Even if life gets busy one thing I can do to take care of myself is:
_____
_____

Feeling Anxious? Did you know that moving your body can help relieve stress? That's right exercise releases endorphins which triggers a positive feeling in the body.

Did you move your body today? (a 20 minute walk counts)

☐   ☐
YES   NO

Reflect

Self Care: Book yourself a mini vacation!

☐ Task Completed

M ☐ T ☐ W ☐ T ☐ F ☐ S ☐ S ☐

DAILY
Check-in

DATE : ____ ____ ____

I am grateful for...
_____
_____
_____
_____

Today I'm proud that I...
_____
_____
_____

How do you feel today?:

- ☐ Happy
- ☐ Sad
- ☐ Stressed
- ☐ Energized
- ☐ Tired
- ☐ Stressed
- ☐ Fearful
- ☐ Angry

- ☐ Peaceful
- ☐ Disappointed
- ☐ Anxious
- ☐ Annoyed
- ☐ Hopeful
- ☐ Calm
- ☐ Productive
- ☐ Excited

- ☐ Negative
- ☐ Strong
- ☐ Inspired
- ☐ Thankful
- ☐ Loving
- ☐ Loved
- ☐ _____
- ☐ _____

What happened?
_____
_____
_____

How have you grown lately?

1. _____
_____
2. _____
_____
3. _____
_____
_____

M T W T F S S
☐ ☐ ☐ ☐ ☐ ☐ ☐

DAILY *Check-in*

DATE : ____ ____ ____

◇◇◇

I am grateful for...
_____
_____
_____
_____

I should listen to my body more when...
_____
_____
_____
_____
_____
_____

I know I am capable of...
_____
_____
_____
_____

What are you looking forward to tomorrow?:
_____
_____
_____
_____

♡ Self Care: Watch one of your favorite movies.

☐ Task Completed

M T W T F S S
☐ ☐ ☐ ☐ ☐ ☐ ☐

DAILY
Check-in

DATE : ____ ____ ____

What is the best thing that happened today or yesterday?

_____
_____
_____
_____

Positive Affirmation: I am...

_____
_____
_____

How do you feel today?:

- ☐ Happy
- ☐ Sad
- ☐ Stressed
- ☐ Energized
- ☐ Tired
- ☐ Stressed
- ☐ Fearful
- ☐ Angry

- ☐ Peaceful
- ☐ Disappointed
- ☐ Anxious
- ☐ Annoyed
- ☐ Hopeful
- ☐ Calm
- ☐ Productive
- ☐ Excited

- ☐ Negative
- ☐ Strong
- ☐ Inspired
- ☐ Thankful
- ☐ Loving
- ☐ Loved
- ☐ _____
- ☐ _____

What happened?

_____
_____
_____

What do you want to celebrate about yourself today?

1. _____
2. _____
3. _____
4. _____

M T W T F S S
☐ ☐ ☐ ☐ ☐ ☐ ☐

DAILY
Check-in

DATE : ___ ___ ___

◊◊

Intention for the day:

_____
_____
_____
_____

How do you maintain balance in your life? Are there any changes you need to make?

_____
_____
_____
_____
_____
_____

What is a habit you would like to change?

_____
_____
_____
_____
_____
_____
_____

What's something that will bring you joy this week?

_____
_____
_____
_____

M T W T F S S
☐ ☐ ☐ ☐ ☐ ☐ ☐

DAILY
Check-in

DATE : ____ ____ ____

> **The power of imagination makes us infinite. - *John Muir***

I am grateful for...
_____
_____
_____

Today I will:
_____
_____
_____
_____

Notes//Reminders

I'm proud of myself for...
_____
_____
_____
_____
_____
_____

M T W T F S S
☐ ☐ ☐ ☐ ☐ ☐ ☐

DAILY
Check-in

DATE : ____ ____ ____

I am grateful for...
_____
_____
_____
_____

How can you help someone else this coming week?
_____
_____
_____
_____
_____

One micro goal that I acomplisehd today:
_____
_____
_____
_____
_____
_____

Big Wins/ Lessons
_____
_____
_____
_____
_____
_____
_____

M T W T F S S
☐ ☐ ☐ ☐ ☐ ☐ ☐

DAILY
Check-in

DATE : ____ ____ ____

> *Success is not final, failure is not fatal: it is the courage to continue that counts. - Winston Churchill*

What can I do right now to make the week less stressful?
_____
_____
_____
_____
_____
_____
_____
_____
_____
_____

Wellness commitment:
This week I will take better care of my body by:
_____
_____
_____

Even if life gets busy one thing I can do to take care of myself is:
_____
_____

How many times did you move your body this week? (a 20 minute walk counts)
_____
_____

Reflect

Self Care Time: Indulge in your full skincare routine.

Task Completed

M ☐ T ☐ W ☐ T ☐ F ☐ S ☐ S ☐

DAILY
Check-in

DATE : ____ ____ ____

∞∞

Today I am grateful for...

_____
_____
_____
_____

Today I'm looking forward to...

_____
_____
_____

How do you feel today?:

☐ Happy   ☐ Peaceful   ☐ Negative
☐ Sad   ☐ Disappointed   ☐ Strong
☐ Stressed   ☐ Anxious   ☐ Inspired
☐ Energized   ☐ Annoyed   ☐ Thankful
☐ Tired   ☐ Hopeful   ☐ Loving
☐ Stressed   ☐ Calm   ☐ Loved
☐ Fearful   ☐ Productive   ☐ _____
☐ Angry   ☐ Excited   ☐ _____

What happened?

_____
_____
_____

Things that went well today?

1. _____
   _____
2. _____
   _____
3. _____
   _____
4. _____
   _____

M T W T F S S
☐ ☐ ☐ ☐ ☐ ☐ ☐

DAILY
Check-in

DATE : ____ ____ ____

I am grateful for...
_____
_____
_____
_____

What is the best advice someone has ever given you? Furthermore, what impact did this have on your life?
_____
_____
_____
_____
_____
_____

What is something you would love to learn how to do?
_____
_____
_____
_____

What are you looking forward to tomorrow?:
_____
_____
_____

♡ Self Care Time: Spend some time alone with yourself to recharge.

☐ Task Completed

M T W T F S S
☐ ☐ ☐ ☐ ☐ ☐ ☐

DAILY
Check-in

DATE : ____ ____ ____

~~~~~~

What is the best thing that happened today or yesterday?
_____
_____
_____
_____

Positive Affirmation: I am...
_____
_____
_____

How do you feel today?:

- ☐ Happy
- ☐ Sad
- ☐ Stressed
- ☐ Energized
- ☐ Tired
- ☐ Stressed
- ☐ Fearful
- ☐ Angry

- ☐ Peaceful
- ☐ Disappointed
- ☐ Anxious
- ☐ Annoyed
- ☐ Hopeful
- ☐ Calm
- ☐ Productive
- ☐ Excited

- ☐ Negative
- ☐ Strong
- ☐ Inspired
- ☐ Thankful
- ☐ Loving
- ☐ Loved
- ☐ _____
- ☐ _____

What happened?
_____
_____
_____

Finish this sentence: "My life would be incomplete without …"

1. _____
2. _____
3. _____
4. _____

M T W T F S S
☐ ☐ ☐ ☐ ☐ ☐ ☐

DAILY
Check-in

DATE : ____ ____ ___

◇◇

Intention for the day:
_____
_____
_____
_____

Write the words you need to hear right now.
_____
_____
_____
_____
_____
_____

When you are feeling down, what picks you up?
_____
_____
_____
_____
_____
_____

What about your work feels real, necessary, or important to you?
_____
_____
_____
_____

M T W T F S S
☐ ☐ ☐ ☐ ☐ ☐ ☐

DAILY
Check-in

DATE : ____ ____ ____

◇◇◇

I am grateful for...
_____
_____
_____

Today I will:
_____
_____
_____
_____

Notes//Reminders

[   ]

How do you like to relax?
_____
_____
_____
_____
_____
_____

M T W T F S S
☐ ☐ ☐ ☐ ☐ ☐ ☐

DAILY
Check-in

DATE : ____ ____ ____

I am grateful for...

_____
_____
_____
_____

What's something that brought you joy today?

_____
_____
_____
_____
_____

One micro goal that I acomplisehd today:

_____
_____
_____
_____
_____
_____

What do you look forward to most in the future?

_____
_____
_____
_____
_____
_____

M T W T F S S
☐ ☐ ☐ ☐ ☐ ☐ ☐

DAILY
Check-in

DATE : ____ ____ ____

❝ **Accept responsibility for your life. Know that it is you who will get you where you want to go, no one else. - Les Brown**

Is there anyone I've been meaning to talk to?
_____
_____
_____
_____
_____
_____
_____
_____
_____
_____

Wellness commitment:
This week I will take better care of my body by:
_____
_____
_____

Even if life gets busy one thing I can do to take care of myself is:
_____
_____
_____
_____
_____

Did you move your body today? (a 20 minute walk counts)
☐   ☐
YES NO

Reflect

Self Care Time: Do or go somewhere completely new.

☐ Task Completed

M T W T F S S
☐ ☐ ☐ ☐ ☐ ☐ ☐

DAILY
Check-in

DATE : ____ ____ ____

I am grateful for...
_____
_____
_____
_____

Today I'm proud that I...
_____
_____
_____

How do you feel today?:

☐ Happy   ☐ Peaceful   ☐ Negative
☐ Sad   ☐ Disappointed   ☐ Strong
☐ Stressed   ☐ Anxious   ☐ Inspired
☐ Energized   ☐ Annoyed   ☐ Thankful
☐ Tired   ☐ Hopeful   ☐ Loving
☐ Stressed   ☐ Calm   ☐ Loved
☐ Fearful   ☐ Productive   ☐ _____
☐ Angry   ☐ Excited   ☐ _____

What happened?
_____
_____
_____

Things that went well today?
1. _____
   _____
2. _____
   _____
3. _____
   _____

M T W T F S S
☐ ☐ ☐ ☐ ☐ ☐ ☐

DAILY
Check-in

DATE : ____ ____ ____

I am grateful for...
_____
_____
_____
_____

What am I holding onto that I need to forgive myself for?
_____
_____
_____
_____
_____
_____

How does it feel to be the age you currently are?
_____
_____
_____
_____
_____
_____
_____
_____

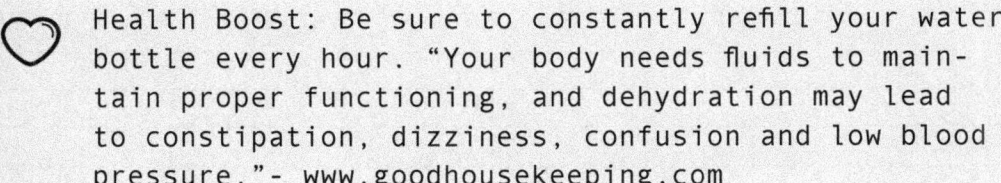

Health Boost: Be sure to constantly refill your water bottle every hour. "Your body needs fluids to maintain proper functioning, and dehydration may lead to constipation, dizziness, confusion and low blood pressure."- www.goodhousekeeping.com

M ☐ T ☐ W ☐ T ☐ F ☐ S ☐ S ☐

DAILY
Check-in

DATE : ____ ____ ____

~~~~~~

What is the best thing that happened today or yesterday?
_____
_____
_____
_____

Positive Affirmation: I am...
_____
_____
_____

How do you feel today?:

- ☐ Happy
- ☐ Sad
- ☐ Stressed
- ☐ Energized
- ☐ Tired
- ☐ Stressed
- ☐ Fearful
- ☐ Angry

- ☐ Peaceful
- ☐ Disappointed
- ☐ Anxious
- ☐ Annoyed
- ☐ Hopeful
- ☐ Calm
- ☐ Productive
- ☐ Excited

- ☐ Negative
- ☐ Strong
- ☐ Inspired
- ☐ Thankful
- ☐ Loving
- ☐ Loved
- ☐ _____
- ☐ _____

What happened?
_____
_____

What is one thing you can do today that will make you feel great?
_____
_____
_____
_____
_____

M T W T F S S
☐ ☐ ☐ ☐ ☐ ☐ ☐

DAILY
Check-in

DATE : _____ _____ _____

Intention for the day:
_____
_____
_____
_____

What do you love about your mind?
_____
_____
_____
_____
_____
_____

What do you love about your personality?
_____
_____
_____
_____
_____
_____
_____
_____

What do you love about your body?
_____
_____
_____
_____
_____

M T W T F S S
☐ ☐ ☐ ☐ ☐ ☐ ☐

DAILY
Check-in

DATE : _____ _____ _____

◇◇

I am grateful for...
_____
_____
_____

Today I will:
_____
_____
_____
_____

Notes//Reminders

How would you like to be remembered?
_____
_____
_____
_____
_____
_____

M T W T F S S
☐ ☐ ☐ ☐ ☐ ☐ ☐

DAILY
Check-in

DATE : ____ ____ ____

I am grateful for...
_____
_____
_____
_____

What do I need more of in my life? Less of?
_____
_____
_____
_____
_____

One micro goal that I acomplisehd today:
_____
_____
_____
_____
_____
_____

How have you changed in the last 5 years?
_____
_____
_____
_____
_____
_____
_____

M T W T F S S
☐ ☐ ☐ ☐ ☐ ☐ ☐

DAILY
Check-in

DATE : ____ ____ ____

> *Someone is sitting in the shade today because someone planted a tree a long time ago. - Warren Buffett*

What limiting beliefs do you have that's keeping you from reaching your dream life?
_____
_____
_____
_____
_____
_____
_____
_____
_____
_____

Wellness commitment:
This week I will take better care of my body by:
_____
_____

Even if life gets busy one thing I can do to take care of myself is:
_____
_____

How many times did you move your body this week? (a 20 minute walk counts)
_____
_____

Reflect

Self Care Time: Make a new playlist for this season of life that'll inspire and make you happy.

☐ Task Completed

M T W T F S S
☐ ☐ ☐ ☐ ☐ ☐ ☐

DAILY
Check-in

DATE : ____ ____ ____

◊◊

Today I am grateful for...
_____
_____
_____
_____

Today I'm looking forward to...
_____
_____
_____

How do you feel today?:

☐ Happy   ☐ Peaceful   ☐ Negative
☐ Sad   ☐ Disappointed   ☐ Strong
☐ Stressed   ☐ Anxious   ☐ Inspired
☐ Energized   ☐ Annoyed   ☐ Thankful
☐ Tired   ☐ Hopeful   ☐ Loving
☐ Stressed   ☐ Calm   ☐ Loved
☐ Fearful   ☐ Productive   ☐ _____
☐ Angry   ☐ Excited   ☐ _____

What happened?
_____
_____
_____

Is there anything that you feel is in the way of your prgress?
_____
_____
_____
_____
_____
_____

M T W T F S S
☐ ☐ ☐ ☐ ☐ ☐ ☐

DAILY
Check-in

DATE : ____ ____ ____

◇◇

I am grateful for...
_____
_____
_____
_____

What are your greatest gifts?
_____
_____
_____
_____
_____
_____
_____

Are you putting any parts of your life on hold? Why?
_____
_____
_____
_____
_____
_____

...How can you start working on that?
_____
_____
_____
_____

♡ Self Care Time: Catch up with a friend or family member you care about.

☐ Task Completed

M ☐ T ☐ W ☐ T ☐ F ☐ S ☐ S ☐

DAILY
Check-in

DATE : ____ ____ ____

◇◇

What is the best thing that happened today or yesterday?
_____
_____
_____
_____

Pick one positive word you'd like to focus on today
_____
_____
_____

How do you feel today?:

- ☐ Happy
- ☐ Sad
- ☐ Stressed
- ☐ Energized
- ☐ Tired
- ☐ Stressed
- ☐ Fearful
- ☐ Angry

- ☐ Peaceful
- ☐ Disappointed
- ☐ Anxious
- ☐ Annoyed
- ☐ Hopeful
- ☐ Calm
- ☐ Productive
- ☐ Excited

- ☐ Negative
- ☐ Strong
- ☐ Inspired
- ☐ Thankful
- ☐ Loving
- ☐ Loved
- ☐ _____
- ☐ _____

What happened?
_____
_____
_____

What do you want to celebrate about yourself today?

1. _____
2. _____
3. _____
4. _____

M T W T F S S
☐ ☐ ☐ ☐ ☐ ☐ ☐

DAILY
Check-in

DATE : ____ ____ ____

Intention for the day:
_____
_____
_____
_____

what drives you?
_____
_____
_____
_____
_____
_____

What empowering beliefs can you take on to help you achieve your goals?
_____
_____
_____
_____
_____
_____
_____

What's something that will bring you joy this week?
_____
_____
_____
_____

M T W T F S S
☐ ☐ ☐ ☐ ☐ ☐ ☐

DAILY
Check-in

DATE : ____ ____ ____

◇◇

I am grateful for...
_____
_____
_____

Today I will:
_____
_____
_____
_____

Notes//Reminders

What do you love about your life?
_____
_____
_____
_____
_____
_____

M T W T F S S
☐ ☐ ☐ ☐ ☐ ☐ ☐

DAILY
Check-in

DATE : ____ ____ ____

I am grateful for...
_____
_____
_____
_____

What excites you about your future?
_____
_____
_____
_____
_____

One micro goal that I acomplisehd today:
_____
_____
_____
_____
_____
_____
_____

What are some good habits that you would like to start?
_____
_____
_____
_____
_____
_____
_____

M T W T F S S
☐ ☐ ☐ ☐ ☐ ☐ ☐

DAILY
Check-in

DATE : ____ ____ ____

> *With self-discipline most anything is possible. - Theodore Roosevelt*

Are you happy with the relationships in your life?
_____
_____
_____
_____
_____
_____
_____
_____
_____
_____

Wellness commitment:
This week I will take better care of my body by:
_____
_____

Even if life gets busy one thing I can do to take care of myself is:
_____
_____

How many times did you move your body this week? (a 20 minute walk counts)
_____
_____

Reflect

www.ingramcontent.com/pod-product-compliance
Lightning Source LLC
Chambersburg PA
CBHW031637160426
43196CB00006B/451